GW01606295

Fra' Tommaso da Celano

THE LIFE OF ST. CLARE VIRGIN

EDITRICE MINERVA
Assisi

Translated from the Italian
by Catherine Bolton Magrini

INDEX

PART ONE

PART TWO

Letter of preface to the text of the Life of St. Clare, Virgin addressed the Supreme Pontiff

Almost as if dissolution were threatening the aged world, the vision of the faithful had dimmed, morals wavered and the courage of manly actions languished: indeed, the accumulation of an age-old way of life was also accompanied by an accumulation of vice. Through the mystery of His mercy, God, who loves mankind, then created two new sacred Orders, upholding the faith and guiding moral reform through them[1]. I would safely dare to say that these modern fathers and their true followers are luminaries of the world, pathfinders, teachers of the way of life, and even though evening was approaching, through them the brilliance of the noonday sun shone over the world so that "he who walked in darkness might see light"[2]. Of course, it would not have been right for the weaker sex not to receive any help because, having fallen into the

[1] This passage parallels the concept set forth in Dante's triplet: "The providence, which doth the world dispose... appointed in her favor captains two" (Par., XI, 28-34), the captains being Francis and Dominic. Here, however, Celano seems to mean Clare rather than Dominic.

[2] See Is 9, 2 and Lk 1, 79.

maelstrom of capriciousness, not only was its voluptuous nature equally as attracted to sin, but indeed, its very fragility pushed it towards sin even more. Thus, the merciful God raised up the venerable virgin Clare and lit the brightest light within her for women to see. Most blessed Pope, compelled by the proof of her miracles, you too have inscribed her name in the catalogue of Saints[3], thereby "setting this lamp on a stand where it gives light to all in the house"[4]. We honor you as Father of these Orders, acknowledge you as their teacher, respect you as their protector and honor you as their master, for although you have taken to heart your concern for the universal guidance of the great ship, you have not neglected to give special and careful attention to the little ship. While it is true that Your Lordship decided to ask this lowly being to examine the Acta of St. Clare[5] and to compile the text for you to read, my lack of literary experience surely would have made me recoil from this task in fear if the pontifical authority had not repeatedly con-

---

[3] While he was still cardinal, Reginald had been named protector of the entire Order of St Damian's by his uncle, Gregory IX. While in this office, he had approved St Clare's Rule and presented it to Innocent IV. As Pope Alexander IV, he canonized her in August of 1255.

[4] Mt 5, 15.

[5] These are the "proceedings" for the cause of canonization.

firmed this request in person. Therefore, since I have set out to complete this commission and did not consider it proper methodology for me to proceed based on the sketchy information I was given to read, I turned to Blessed Francis' companions[6] and to the community of Christ's virgins itself, often reflecting deep in my heart over the precept that it would not be acceptable to weave this story authoritatively without consulting eye witnesses or people who had been informed by eye witnesses. In fear of the Lord, I am repeating in full what I have learned from them, sticking to the truth. Thus, after gathering some information and omitting even more, I have set down this information with a smooth and fluent pen so that, since this story of the virgin's marvels is intended for the delight of virgins, a mind that has not been refined by culture will not be muddled by tortuous language. Thus, let men follow those men who are new disciples of the Word made flesh and let women imitate Clare, follower of the Mother of God and new leader of women[7]. Most holy Father, just as you have full authority in this matter to correct, delete and make additions, my will is likewise completely subject to

[6] Clare was survived by two of Francis' disciples, Brother Angelo, Minister of Umbria, and Brother Leo, both of whom took part in the canonization proceedings.

[7] In Franciscan spirituality, Clare's special task was to imitate Mary, just as Francis had imitated Christ.

yours, identical to yours and pleased by yours. May the Lord Jesus Christ grant you prosperity now and in the future. Amen.

PART ONE

Here begins the text of the Life of St. Clare, Virgin

First of all, about her birth.

The marvelous woman of the city of Assisi, Clare in both name and virtue[1], came from a very distinguished family. First she was Blessed Francis' fellow citizen on earth and then his fellow sovereign in heaven. Her father was a nobleman and the entire lineage on both sides of the family came from knightly aristocracy. Their house was well-stocked and they were wealthy in all things that were considered riches in the land in which they lived. Her mother, named Ortolana[2], who was to give birth to a fruitful little plant in the garden of the Church, was rich in good fruits herself. In fact, although she had been placed under the bonds of matrimony and had to tend to the needs of her family, she nevertheless dedicated herself to the best of her ability to divine worship and often did works of charity.

---

[1] The Italian name for Clare, "Chiara", is derived from the adjective "chiaro", which has several meanings – clear, unclouded, bright, renowned. Hence the dual significance of her name.

[2] In Italian, the word "ortolana" means lady gardener.

After she piously made a pilgrimage abroad and visited those places that the Son of Man had blessed with his sacred footsteps, she was filled with joy when she finally returned home. Subsequently, she went to the shrine of St. Michael the Archangel[3] to pray and she reverently visited the threshold of the Apostles.

2. What more can be said? You can tell a tree by its fruit[4], while the fruit itself draws its value from the tree. A copy of divine blessing preceded in the root so that an abundance of saintliness could emerge in its buds[5]. At last, the pregnant woman, who was approaching childbirth by this time, was in church praying intently before the cross to ask Christ Crucified to bring her safely through the dangers of childbirth when she heard a voice saying to her[6] "Woman, fear not, for safe and sound you shall give birth to a light that will greatly illuminate the world"[7]. Enlightened by this prophesy, when

---

[3] In the Gargano area of southern Italy. St Francis was also very devoted to St Michael.

[4] Mt 12, 33.

[5] Celano continues his metaphorical reference to Clare as "a little plant in the garden of the church" who was planted there by her mother, Ortolana (see note 2 above).

[6] Acts 9, 4.

[7] By ordering Francis to restore the church of St Damian, the Crucifix had preordained the reforms that would later be extended throughout the Catholic Church. Likewise, the Crucifix spoke to Ortolana, presaging the life of St Clare, who was

her baby was reborn in holy baptism, she chose to call her Clare in the hopes that, through divine will, she would somehow achieve the brightness of that promised light.

Of the lifestyle in her father's house[8].

Shortly after she was born, little Clare began to shine through the mundane shadows with a highly precocious brilliance and even at a very tender age, she started to glow through the integrity of her behavior. First of all, she meekly received her first lessons in the faith directly from her mother's lips. By teaching her and shaping her from within, that truly pure vessel of the Holy Spirit proved itself to be a vessel of grace. "She willingly extended her arms to the needy and took from the abundance of her own house in order to compensate for the poverty of many"[9]. In order to render her sacrifice even more pleasing to God, she made her own little body go without many delicacies, secretly sending them through her appointees to nourish the bellies of the

---

highly devoted to the Crucifix. Ortolana herself recounted this prophesy to Sister Cecilia of Spello (*Proceedings for the Canonization of St Clare*).

[8] Clare's family home was located next to the Cathedral of San Rufino.

[9] See Prv 31, 20 and 2 Cor 8, 14.

weak[10]. Thus, since mercy had grown within her right from infancy, she was compassionate in spirit and took pity on the misery of the wretched.

4. She delighted in attending holy prayer regularly and because she was surrounded so often by the sweet fragrance of prayer, little by little she attained a heavenly life. Since she did not have a string of beads on which to count her Our Fathers, she used a small pile of pebbles to keep track of her little prayers to the Lord. Beginning to feel the initial flow of divine love, she felt it was her duty to turn her back on the fickle colors of the flower of worldly pleasure and, through the blessing of the Holy Spirit, she was taught to attach little value to worthless objects. Consequently, she wore a little hair shirt beneath her soft and precious clothing [11], thus giving the world the appearance of being adorned on the outside but clothing herself with Christ on the inside[12].

When at last her family wished her to enter a noble marriage, she never consented but, by pretending to postpone her marriage to a mortal to some future date, she commended her virginity to the Lord.

These are a few examples of the virtue she

---

[10] See Jb 31.

[11] See Lk 7, 25.

[12] Rom 13, 14 and Gal 3, 27.

demonstrated while in her father's house. These were the early fruits of her spirit and the signs of her holiness. Thus, abounding in such intense perfumes[13], she was like a storeroom of fragrances that, although well sealed, gives itself away through its very scent. Although she was unaware of it, in fact, her neighbors began to speak her praises and once her secret works were revealed by truthful renown, the word of her goodness spread throughout the populace.

---

[13] The "perfume" referred to here is saintliness itself. Celano uses this image repeatedly.

Of her acquaintance and friendship with Blessed Francis.

5. At this point, as soon as she heard the praise being given to Francis who, like a new man and through new virtues, was renewing the way of perfection that had been lost to the world, she immediately wished to hear him speak and to see him. She had been persuaded to do this by God the Father, who had already given both Francis and Clare their initial impetus[14], although in different ways. And as the fame of this lovely young girl had already reached Francis as well, his desire to see her and to talk to her was no less intense. Since he had come to destroy the reign of worldly pleasures, he was so dedicated to winning his plunder that he hoped he could snatch this noble prize from the world somehow and claim her for his Lord. He visited the girl and, more often than not, she visited him[15], spacing the time intervals between their vis-

---

[14] Francis had already abandoned his worldly life to take on a life of penance and apostolate and, in fact, had disciples as early as the year 1209.

[15] According to the testimony of Beatrice, St Clare's sister, Francis was the one who made the first visit (*Proceedings*, XVII).

its so that this divine attraction could not humanly be perceived by anyone or harmed by public gossip.

Thus, accompanied by only one person she knew[16], the girl left her ancestral palace and secretly went to the man of God, whose words were like fire to her and whose works seemed superhuman. Father Francis urged her to turn her back on the world, using vivid language to show her how arid temporal hope is and how deceptive it can appear. He instilled in her the sweetness of marriage to Christ, convincing her to protect the gem of virginal purity for that blessed Bridegroom who had been made man through love.

6. Why linger over words ? Upon the request of this most holy father and at his zealous urging, the virgin did not hesitate to give her consent like a most faithful bridesmaid. Comprehension of this eternal joy dawned on her immediately, so that the whole world became worthless in comparison. She was consumed by her desire for this joy and, out of love for this joy, she yearned for this sublime marriage.

And in fact, kindled by a celestial flame, she spurned temporal vainglory so supremely that she no longer felt any attraction in her heart for worldly

---

[16] Specifically, Bona of Guelfuccio, one of Clare's relatives, stated that she had accompanied Clare several times to speak with Francis. Brother Philip was also present several times (*Proceedings*, XVII).

splendor. In addition, detesting all temptation of the flesh, she now resolved that she would never know any "transgression of the marriage bed"[17], because she wished to make her body a temple only for God and she worked diligently to make herself worthy of this union with the great King through her virtue. At this point, she entrusted herself completely to Francis' judgment, choosing him as her guide on the path she was to follow, second only to God. By now, her soul was dependent on his sacred counsel and she welcomed to her blazing soul everything he revealed to her through his words about sweet Jesus. By this time, the elegance of mundane adornments annoyed her and, in order to gain Christ, she considered as dung all things[18] that were cause for admiration in the outside world.

---

[17] Wis 3, 13.
[18] Phil 3, 8.

How, through Blessed Francis' help, she went from secular to religious life.

7. In order to keep the mirror of her immaculate mind from being tarnished by worldly dust and to prevent the contagion of secular life from growing in that pure young girl, her pious father soon hastened to lead Clare out of temporal darkness. When the solemn celebration of Palm Sunday was approaching[19], this young girl eagerly went to visit the man of God to ask him about when and how this change in her life was going to take place. Father Francis ordered her to dress up in all her finery and to go up with the throng to receive the palm frond on that feast day. Then, the following evening she was to "go outside the camp" [20] to turn worldly joy into sorrow over the Lord's Passion[21]. Therefore, the young girl, radiant in her festive splendor, entered the church that Sunday together with a

---

[19] There seems to be some discrepancy as to the exact date: according to some historians, it was March 28, 1211, whereas others cite March 18, 1212.

[20] This expression drawn from Paul's letter to the Hebrews (13, 13), with its bellicose overtones, is particularly apt here as it illustrates the concept of the struggle that is necessary to achieve victory.

[21] Jas 4, 9.

group of other ladies and a fitting omen occurred at this point. While the others ran forward to get their olive branches, Clare reticently remained motionless in her place instead. The bishop[22] came down the steps towards her and placed the palm right into her hands. The following night, after she had prepared herself according to Saint Francis' orders, she made her desired escape together with honorable company[23]. Since she did not think it would be wise to leave through the usual door, using her bare hands with a strength that seemed extraordinary even to her, she managed to open a different door that had been blocked off with wooden planks and heavy rocks.

8. Thus, having abandoned her house, her city and her family, she hurried towards St. Mary's of the Porziuncola where the brothers, who were holding a prayer vigil before God's little altar, welcomed the virgin Clare with candles. There, leaving the filth of Babylon behind her, she renounced the world[24]. There, letting the brothers cut off her

---

[22] The bishop referred to here was Guido II and the church was the Cathedral of San Rufino.

[23] She was not accompanied by Bona, who had gone on a pilgrimage, but was joined either by one of Guelfuccio's other daughters, Pacifica, who then became one of Clare's first disciples, or by a different unnamed person.

[24] Dt 24, 1.

hair[25], she abandoned her colorful baubles. Indeed, at the twilight of that age, it would not have been fitting for the Order of flowering virginity to be born anywhere else but in the court of the Lady who, before all other women and more worthy than all others, was the only woman to become a mother yet remain a virgin. This is the place in which, under Francis' command, the new army of the poor[26] had its happy beginnings. Thus, it is plain to see that the merciful Mother gave birth to both religious Orders in her own house. Then, as soon as this humble maiden had accepted the emblems of holy penance before Blessed Mary's altar and had been united to Christ virtually in front of this Virgin's marriage bed, St Francis immediately led her to the Church of St Paul[27], where she was to live until God gave them new orders.

How she firmly resisted her family's assault.

9. Just as soon her family heard the news, however, they broken-heartedly condemned the virgin's

---

[25] The *Cause of Canonization* clearly states that she "received the tonsure" from St Francis.

[26] This term could be understood to mean both the male and female orders, referring to the First and Second Orders.

[27] This was the church of the Benedictine monastery in Bastia Umbra, about 5 kilometers from Assisi.

actions and intentions and joined together to rush over to that place in an attempt to obtain the impossible. They tried violence, venomous counsel and bland promises in order to convince her to withdraw from such a lowly state[28], which not only went against her noble birth but which was not even validated by any other examples in the area. Nevertheless, clinging to the altar linens, she bared her tonsured head and declared that she would never allow herself to be torn away from serving Christ[29]. As her family's struggle against her grew stronger and stronger, so did her courage, and the love that was awakened in her by their insults gave her strength. Things went on like this for many days and although she was kept from the way of the Lord and her family opposed her saintly intentions, her soul never wavered and her ardor did not diminish. Instead, amidst their offensive words and their spitefulness, she tempered her soul with hope and her relatives, having been rejected, finally gave in and were appeased.

---

[28] To them, Clare could almost have appeared to be like a humble oblate monastic sister.

[29] See the *Cause of Canonization*. According to this source, however, her relatives' assault did not take place at St Paul's but at St Angelo of Panzo. This scene is depicted in one of the eight stories on the table painted in 1283 in the Basilica of St Clare.

10. A few days later, she went to the church of St Angelo of Panzo[30]. However, since her heart could not rest easily there, Blessed Francis decided to move her to the church of St Damian's. Here, mooring the anchor of her mind in a safe harbor, she was no longer tossed about by her moves from place to place. She had no doubts about poverty, nor was she frightened by solitude. This was the church that Francis had so zealously labored to restore[31] and he had even offered money to the priest of this church to pay for the restoration work. This is the church in which a voice had descended from the wooden crucifix while Francis was praying, telling him, "Go, Francis, repair my house which, as you can see is in ruins"[32]. Out of love for her heavenly Bridegroom, the virgin Clare locked herself into the prison of this little place. Hiding herself from the tempestuous world, she incarcerated her body here for the rest of her life. Making her silver nest in the clefts of these rocks, the dove gave birth to a college of virgins of Christ, founded a holy monastery and started the Order of the Poor Clares. This is where she broke her body in penance, where she sowed the seeds of perfect justice and where her footsteps marked the path for her

---

[30] Located on the slopes of Mount Subasio, near Assisi, and not within the city walls.

[31] See Thomas of Celano, *First Life*.

[32] See Thomas of Celano, *Second Life*.

followers. Within this harsh cloister, she broke the alabaster of her very body with the scourge of discipline for forty-two years so that the house of the Church would be filled with the scent of this perfume. However, we can't offer proof of how gloriously she lived there until we have recounted the number of great souls who came to Christ through her work and who they were.

How the fame of her virtues spread far and wide

Indeed, shortly thereafter, the news of the virgin Clare's saintliness spread throughout the areas nearby and women came from all parts to pursue "the scent of her perfume"[33]. Following her example, virgins hastened to keep themselves pure for Christ, married women tried to live more chastely and famous and noble people, abandoning their comfortable palaces, built lowly monasteries for themselves[34] and considered it a great honor to live "in a sackcloth and ashes"[35] out of love for Christ. Even the lustiness of young men was impelled to compete in these contests of purity and the strong examples set by the weaker sex incited these youths to abandon the fickle ways of the flesh. Lastly, many people who were already united in matrimony mutually consented to commit themselves to abstinence, the husbands entering the Orders and their

---

[33] Sg 1, 3.

[34] Many of Clare's first followers at St Damian's – her own sister for example – came from noble families. Others include Philippa, daughter of Leonard of Gislerio and Agnes of Prague, daughter of the King of Bohemia.

[35] Mt 11, 21.

wives the monasteries[36]. Mothers invited their daughters to Christ and daughters their mothers, sister attracted sister to Christ and aunts their nieces[37]. In eager emulation, they all wished to serve Christ. All of them wanted to participate in this angelic life that Clare was illustrating to them. Moved by Clare's fame, countless virgins who could not commit themselves to cloistered life tried to follow the spirit of the Rule[38] at home, even though they were not bound by any rules. Through her example, the virgin Clare sowed so many great seeds of salvation that she seemed to fulfill the prophecy that "more numerous are the children of the deserted wife than the children of her who has a husband".

How the news of her goodness even reached women far away.

11. In the meantime, in order to keep the source of this heavenly blessing that rises in the

---

[36] This appears to be a reference to men who took Holy Orders or entered the Order of the Friars Minor, and not a reference to the Third Order Secular.

[37] Celano is alluding to Ortolana, Clare's mother, and to Agnes and Beatrice, her sisters, as well as to Balvina of Corano and Amata, the saint's nieces.

[38] The Rule of St Clare.

Spoleto valley from being confined within limited boundaries, it was transformed into a wide current so that its "runlets might gladden the city of God"[39]. In fact, the novelty of these great events spread far and wide to all parts and began to gain souls everywhere for Christ. Even though she was confined, Clare began to spread a ray of light throughout the world and she shone brightly through this well-deserved praise. The fame of her virtue filled the halls of illustrious men. It reached the palaces of duchesses and even penetrated the recesses of queens. The highest nobility bent down to follow in her footsteps and, through sacred humility, turned away from the haughty ancestry of its blood. Beckoned by these tributes to Clare, some women who were worthy of marriage to dukes and kings underwent harsh penance[40] and those who had already married powerful men imitated Clare in their own way. Countless cities[41] were embel-

---

[39] Ps 46, 5.

[40] Agnes, daughter of the King of Bohemia, could not be convinced by either her father or her brother to marry Emperor Frederick II, nor King Henry III of England. She became a Poor Clare around 1236 and lived in the monastery she herself founded in Prague. Also Isabelle of France, sister of Louis IX who was later canonized a saint, refused to agree to marry Conrad, son of Emperor Frederick, although Pope Innocent IV himself requested it.She founded the monastery of Longchamp around 1255.

[41] This is no exaggeration. By August 18, 1228, there were

lished with monasteries and even country and mountain areas were beautified by the construction of these celestial buildings. With holy Clare paving the way, the cult of chastity multiplied throughout the world and the state of virginity was revived and came into vogue. Today, the Church flourishes happily with the blessed flowers that Clare produced: this is the Church that had asked to be sustained, saying, "strengthen me with flowers, refresh me with apples, for I am faint with love"[42].

But now, let this pen return to its task so that Clare's way of life can be made known.

---

at least 24 monasteries under the jurisdiction of Cardinal Reginald.In fact, some cities had more than one monastery and monasteries were also build across the Alps and overseas.

[42] Sg 2, 5.

Of her blessed humility.

12. This woman, cornerstone and noble foundation of her Order[43], strove from the very start to erect the structure of complete virtue over the foundation of her blessed humility. Indeed, she promised holy obedience to Blessed Francis and never strayed from this promise[44]. For three years following her conversion, she turned down the title and office of abbess, humbly preferring to be placed in a subordinate position rather than at the head, and she was more willing to serve among Christ's handmaidens than be served. After that, St Francis compelled her to assume the leadership of these Women, but instead of breeding arrogance in her heart, this office bread fear in her, and rather than giving her a greater amount of freedom, it made her even more submissive. The higher up she appeared to be on account of this great semblance of superiority, the lower her self-esteem, the more

---

[43] This is how she is defined in the *Cause of Canonization*. Thus, she is recognized implicitly as Founder of the Order or in any case, as Co-founder.

[44] In her Rule, St Clare emphasizes her willingness to obey the Pope and St Francis, as well as their successors.

willing to do her duty and the viler her outward appearance became. She would no longer refuse to do any servile task, so that most of the time, she was the one who poured water over her sisters' hands, remained standing while they were seated and served food while they ate[45]. She was very unwilling to give any orders and carried them out herself instead, preferring to do things on her own rather than ordering the sisters to do them. She washed the chamber pots of the sisters who were ill: she who was so noble in spirit rinsed them out without recoiling from the filth or being disgusted by the stench. She often washed the feet of the servants who were returning from outside and after she had finished washing them, she kissed them.

Once she was washing a servant's feet and as she was about to kiss them, the woman, who could not bear the sight of such humiliation, yanked her foot away, hitting her lady on the face. Clare, however, sweetly took the servant's foot and firmly planted a kiss on her sole.

---

[45] Clare's attitude demonstrates that she was truly indifferent to any deference that may have been due her. Instead, she attempted to establish equality among the sisters.

Of the saint and true poverty.

13. She reconciled her poverty in all worldly goods with spiritual poverty, which is true humility. First of all, when she first converted her way of life, she sold the inheritance she had received from her father[46] and gave everything away to the poor without keeping anything for herself. From this point on, since she had left the world behind her and had enriched her inner spirit, she was freed of all burdens and could follow Christ without any baggage[47]. Lastly, she made such a strong covenant with blessed poverty and bound herself to it with such love that she wanted to possess nothing but Christ the Lord and would not allow her daughters to own anything either. She believed that it was impossible to cherish "the very precious pearl" of heavenly desire, which is "bought by selling everything"[48], while also maintaining an all-consuming preoccupation with worldly goods. Through her frequent exhortations to her sisters, she taught them

---

[46] Whether or not Favarone was still alive when Clare took the veil is still being debated. If she had already been orphaned by 1211 when she converted, then she had already received her inheritance. Otherwise, she received it after she had already become a nun once her father passed away. In any case, she gave away her entire inheritance.

[47] Lk 10, 4.

[48] Mt 13, 46.

that their community would only be acceptable to God when it was rich in poverty and that it would last solidly through eternity only if it were defended at all times by the tower of sublime poverty. She urged them, in their little nest of poverty, to conform to poor Christ who, as a tiny baby, had been placed in a wretched manger by His poor Mother[49]. Indeed, recalling this particular event and holding onto it almost as if it were a golden necklace, she beat her breast so that the dust of worldly desire could not make its way in.

14. Since she wanted her religious family to gain the title of poverty, she petitioned Innocent III for the privilege of poverty. Delighted by the virgin's great devotion, this wonderful man took note of the uniqueness of her proposal, since a privilege of this sort had never been requested before at the Holy See. In order to ensure that such an unusual petition would be smiled upon by unusual favor, it was with great joy that the Pontiff himself wrote the draft of the requested diploma in his own hand. Pope Gregory, a man who was not only very worthy of the papal chair but who was also respected through personal merit, dearly loved this saint like a father. Although he tried to persuade her to agree to own some property, freely offering it to her himself, Clare very courageously objected and refused

---

[49] Lk 2, 7.

to consent to this[50]. Hence, when the Pontiff said to her, "We will absolve you of your vow if that is what you are afraid of," she replied, "Holy Father, on no account do I wish to be dispensed forever from following Christ"!

She very cheerfully received donated scraps and crumbs of bread brought by the mendicant friars, becoming practically despondent at the sight of entire loaves of bread and rejoicing instead over the scraps. Why mince words? She dedicated herself to conforming to our poor Crucified Christ in utmost poverty, so that no fleeting thing could separate the lover from her Beloved or keep her from her journey with the Lord.

Thus, I have been told about two miracles that this lover of poverty was able to work.

---

[50] Sister Pacifica, Sister Benvenuta and Sister Philippa testified to Clare's firm but respectful stance towards the Pope (*Proceedings*).

The miracle of the multiplication of the loaves.

15. There was only one loaf of bread left in the monastery, but pangs of hunger as well as the dinner hour were both upon them. The sister in charge of the pantry called the Saint, who ordered her to divide the bread and send part of it to the friars, keeping the rest for the sisters. Then she ordered her to slice the remaining half into fifty pieces, which was the number of women there, and to place the slices before them on the table of poverty. The devoted sister replied, "We would need the ancient miracles of Christ to turn such a small amount of bread into fifty slices," but her Mother answered her, "Go, daughter, and faithfully do as I say." The daughter rushed off to carry out her Mother's orders, whereas the Mother prayed piously to her Lord on her daughters' behalf. Through divine intervention, that paltry amount grew in the hands of the woman who was breaking it and there was an abundant portion for each member of the community.

Another miracle of the divine gift of the oil.

16. One day, Christ's handmaidens had so little oil that there wasn't even any left to use as a condiment for the sisters who were ill. The lady Clare took a jar and, being a master of humility, rinsed it out with her own hands. She placed the empty container outside where the beggar friar could get it, and then called him so he could go get some oil. It did not take the devoted friar long to come to the aid of such indigence and he ran over to get the jar. "So it is not a question of man's willing or doing but of God's mercy"[51]. In fact, that jar was filled with oil through God's influence alone, for holy Clare's entreaty had preceded the friar's service in helping the poor sisters. Thinking however that he had been called for no reason, this friar murmured under his breath, "These women called me so they could play a practical joke on me, because look! The jar is full!"

Of her mortification of the flesh.

17. Perhaps it would be better for me to remain silent about her admirable mortification of the flesh, for she did such great penance that all

---

[51] Rom 9, 16.

those who hear about it are so amazed that it is difficult for them to accept the reality of these events. The fact that she used a simple little cowl and a poor mantle made of rough cloth, more to cover her delicate body than keep it warm, is no great feat, nor should anyone be amazed that she made absolutely no use of shoes. It was no big thing that she fasted continuously, whatever the season, nor that she slept on a little bed without a feather mattress. In fact, perhaps she does not deserve this praise that she is given, since there were others just like her in this cloister who practiced these same mortifications.

But what affinity could there have been between virginal flesh and porcine clothing? In fact, this holy virgin had obtained a pigskin garment and wore it secretly beneath her cowl, turning the raggedly-cut bristles against her skin. Sometimes she used a stiff hair shirt woven from horsehair with knots all over it, which she cinched against her with rough cords. One time, she lent it to one of her daughters who had requested it, but as soon as this daughter put it on, she was overcome immediately by its roughness and did not ask for it again as happily as she returned it three days later[52]. The naked

[52] Agnes of Oportulo was the one who borrowed Clare's cilice, or hair shirt (Proceedings). Sister Benvenuta and Sister Philippa also testified to this austerity. The hair shirt can still

ground and vine-branches sometimes served as her bed and a hard piece of wood took the place of a pillow beneath her head. Subsequently, in fact, since her body had become weaker, she stretched a mat out on the ground and kindly gave her head some straw on which to rest. In the end, since prolonged illness overcame the body she had treated so harshly, St Francis ordered her to use a bag stuffed with straw.

18. Her abstinence in fasting was also so severe that if she had not been sustained by supernatural virtue, she would barely have survived physically on the scanty sustenance she took. As long as she was healthy, she fasted on bread and water during Lent and during the quadragesima of St Martin (Bishop), only sipping a bit of wine on Sundays if there was any available. And so that you, dear reader, can admire what you yourself would be unable to imitate, three days a week during those Lenten periods, and that is on Monday, Wednesday and Friday, she ate no food at all. Thus, her days of spare meals were alternated with days of harsh penance, so that on the eve of complete starvation, she virtually feasted on a banquet of bread and water. It is no wonder that such great harshness, observed

---

be seen today among the relics exhibited at the Protomonastery: it is a rectangle of fabric made of brown horsehair and stitched together with lighter-colored thread and cording.

over a long period of time, made Clare prone to illness, consumed her strength and enervated her physical vigor. Therefore, this holy Mother's highly devoted children suffered for her and they tearfully deplored those deaths that she willingly succumbed to every day. In the end, Blessed Francis and the Bishop of Assisi forbade St Clare to sustain that ruinous three-day fast, ordering her not to let a day go by without eating at least an ounce and a half of bread[53]. And while serious mortification of the body usually generates spiritual affliction, the opposite was seen in Clare.

In fact, she maintained a festive and joyful outlook through each mortification[54], so that she did not appear to feel any physical anguish but laughed at it instead. It can be understood from this, beyond any shadow of a doubt, that the saintly happiness that filled her from within spilled over to the outside, since the love in her heart removed all the harshness from the scourges inflicted on her body.

---

[53] This took place around 1220.

[54] This is a recurrent Franciscan theme. It was important that fasting be a joyous sacrifice.

Of the practice of holy prayer.

19. Therefore, as if dead to her bodily needs before her time, she was completely foreign to the world and continuously kept her soul occupied in holy prayer and divine praise. This most fervent view of eternal desire had already made her turn towards the light, and like the one who had transcended the sphere of earthly trappings, she opened the innermost part of her mind even further to the showers of grace. For long stretches of time after Complines[55] she prayed with her sisters and as rivers of tears burst forth from her, they were also aroused in the others. Furthermore, after the others sisters had gone to rest their tired bones on their hard pallets and drowsiness had overcome them, she continued to pray, wide awake and indomitable, to welcome stealthily the divinely whispered word[56]. She very often prostrated herself during prayer and, with her face turned towards the ground, she bathed the floor with her tears and

[55] This is the last of the seven canonical hours. It is recited at the end of the day to ask God to keep watch during the night.

[56] See Jb 4, 12.

grazed it with her kisses, so that she always seemed to be holding her Lord, whose feet she would kiss and wash with her tears. Once, as she wept during the dead of night, the angel of darkness appeared to her in the form of a black child who scolded her, "Don't weep so much or you will go blind". She immediately responded, "Anyone who shall see God will not be blinded," and the boy left in confusion. That same night after Matins[57] as Clare was praying bathed in her usual streams of tears, this fraudulent counselor approached her, repeating, "Don't cry so much or your brain will dissolve and run down your nostrils and then your nose will be crooked". And at her quick answer that "no crookedness is suffered by those who serve the Lord", he immediately ran off and disappeared.

20. The amount of support she received in the kiln of ardent prayer and how sweet divine goodness was to her in that sacred fruition can be proven by numerous signs. In fact, whenever she returned joyfully from holy prayer, she brought such warm words with her from the fire of the Lord's altar that they kindled courage in her sisters, who noted in admiration that there was a sort of sweetness radiating from her face and that her countenance was brighter than usual. "Certainly in

---

[57] At that time, the old practice of reciting Matins in the middle of the night was followed.

his sweetness God had set a banquet for the poor woman"[58] and after this true light had filled her mind during prayer, He gave outward manifestations of this light so it could be perceived by the senses as an example. Therefore, inseparably united to her noble Bridegroom in this fleeting world, she constantly delighted in celestial things. In this way, she was sustained by stable virtues in the changeable heavens and kept a treasure of glory enclosed in a fragile clay vase. With her body she resided down on earth, but with her intellect she dwelt in the highest reaches of heaven.

At Matins, she usually awoke before the young girls, whom she silently roused with gestures, inviting them to praise God. She often lit the lanterns while the others slept and rang the bell with her own hands. There was no room for half-heartedness or sluggishness in her cloister, where laziness was routed through a stinging exhortation to pray and serve the Lord.

---

[58] Ps 97, 11.

Of the marvels of her prayers and in particular, of the Saracens who miraculously turned and fled.

21. At this point, with the most scrupulous truthfulness, which is equivalent to proper veneration, I would like to relate the magnificent results of her prayers. During those times in which the Church was being persecuted in various parts of the world at the hands of Emperor Frederick[59], the Spoleto valley[60] drank more and more frequently from the cup of anger[61]. By imperial command, ranks of horsemen and Saracen slingsmen[62] had established themselves there like swarms of bees with the intention of devastating the local encampments and overcoming its cities. At a certain point, the enemy's fury was turned against Assisi, which is one of the Lord's special cities, and as they were nearing her gates, the Saracens, a mean people who thirst for Christian blood and attempt even the most brazen atrocities, poured into St Damian's,

---

[59] This occurred during the papacy of Gregory IX. According to the *Proceedings*, this episode took place one Friday in September, 1240.

[60] The Spoleto valley stretches from the city of Spoleto to Perugia, along the old Roman *iter*, the Flaminian Way.

[61] Rev 14, 10.

[62] Frederick II had Tartars as well as Saracens in his army.

even going within its confines and entering the cloister of the virgins. The virgins were practically faint with fear and, stammering in horror, they went wailing to their Mother. Undaunted, she ordered that they bring her, sick as she was, to the front door and place her before the enemy, carrying the ivory-encased silver box in which they devoutly kept the Body of the Holy of Holies.

22. As soon as she was completely prostrated in prayer to the Lord, she tearfully said to her Christ, "O my Lord, do you want to let your poor servants, whom you raised in your love, fall into the hands of pagans? Lord, I beg you to watch over your servants, whom I cannot defend now on my own." The child-like voice of the propitiator of new grace immediately resounded in her ears: "I will always defend you." "My Lord", she resumed, "also watch over this town that provides for us out of love for You." And Christ answered her, "It will sustain some damage, but my protection will defend her." Then the virgin raised her tearstained face and comforted the weeping women, saying, "My daughters; I faithfully assure you that you will suffer no ill. Just place your trust in Christ!" Nor was there any delay! The audacity of those dogs was immediately replaced with astonishment and, thrown into confusion by that petitioner's courage, they quickly cleared away from the walls they had scaled. Clare instantly warned those who had heard this voice,

"My dearest children, be sure at all costs not to tell anyone about that voice for as long as I live."

Yet another miracle that liberated the city.

23. On another occasion, Vitale d'Anversa, a man who was avid for glory and courageous in battle, moved against Assisi with the army he captained. Consequently, he stripped the region of trees, devastated all the surrounding areas and then began his assault on the city. He menacingly declared that he would never withdraw until he had occupied the very city itself. Things were already at the point that it was feared the city would fall at any time. As soon as she heard about this, however, Clare, servant of Christ, wailed loudly and called her sisters about her, saying, "My dearest daughters, every day we receive many goods from this city. It would be very impious of us not to help her to the best of our ability when the time comes." She ordered her sisters to bring her some ashes and to uncover their heads. After she had bared her own head, first she sprinkled many ashes over it and then she placed some ashes on their heads as well. She continued, "Go to our Lord and ask Him with all your heart to free the city." Why go into all the details? Why recall the tears of the virgins and their intense prayers? The following morning, our merciful God showed them "a way out of the or-

deal"[63] so that, his entire army disbanded, the proud man withdrew against his will and the city was no longer oppressed by him. In fact, this very same condottiere[64] of war was slain by the sword just a short time later.

[63] . I Cor 10, 13.

[64] During the Middle Ages, a "condottiere" was the leader of a mercenary army.

Of the efficacy of her prayer in converting her sister-german[65]

24. It would not be right to bury in silence the miraculous effects of her prayer, which at the dawn of her own conversion[66] also converted one of the first souls to God and then protected it after its conversion[67]. In fact, Clare had a very young sister who was german to her by birth and in purity. In Clare's desire to convert her, one of the first fruits of the prayers she offered to God with complete love was her increasingly insistent request that, just as she had been spiritually attached to her sister while in the world, they also be alike in their willingness to serve God. Therefore, she immediately prayed to the merciful Father and asked Him to make the world displeasing to her sister Agnes, who had been left at home, so that God would become sweet to her, and to change her mind from the idea of carnal marriage to union in His own love. In this

[65] The author repeatedly uses the term "sister german" in order to avoid any confusion that could arise from the double significance of "sister" (sibling) and "sister" (nun). The term "german" means "having the same parents".

[66] This refers to her passage from secular to religious life.

[67] Celano often repeats the same word throughout a sentence for emphasis.

Assisi, The Basilica of St. Francis, Simone Martini, St. Clare

Assisi, San Damiano, The Cloister

Assisi, The Basilica of St. Clare

Assisi, The Basilica of St. Clare, Maestro di St. Chiara, plate with a scene of the life of St. Clare

Assisi, The Basilica of St. Clare, Maestro di St. Chiara, plate with a scene of the life of St. Clare, St. Francis welcomes St. Clare near the Portiuncola

Assisi, The Basilica of St. Clare, Maestro di St. Chiara, plate with a scene of the life of St. Clare. St. Clare's hair is cut by St. Francis

Assisi, The Basilica of St. Clare, Maestro di St. Chiara, plate with a scene of the life of St. Clare, Followers of St. Clare

Assisi, The Basilica of St. Clare, Chapel of St. George, Puccio Capanna, Virgin and St. Clare, detail

way, together with Clare, Agnes would be united with the Bridegroom of glory in perpetual virginity. In fact, the marvelous mutual love that was deeply rooted within both of them had made their unusual separation painful for both of them, although for different reasons. Our Holy Lord promptly helped this extraordinary oratress and quickly granted the first gift that she had requested in particular and that God was most pleased to offer her. In fact, sixteen days after Clare's consecration, Agnes was inspired by the Holy Spirit to hurry off to join her sister, and after revealing her secret desire, she declared that she wished to serve God in all things. Clare joyfully embraced and said, "My dearest sister, I thank God for listening to me in my concern over you."

25. This marvelous conversion was followed by a most admirable defense. In fact, while the happy sisters were at the church of St Angelo of Panzo following in Christ's footsteps and the sister who was knowledgeable in the Lord was teaching her novice and sister-german, a new assault was mounted suddenly against the girls by their family. The very next day after they heard that Agnes had gone to be with Clare, twelve men dashed to the monastery fuming in rage. Outwardly concealing their evil intent, they feigned a peaceful visit. Then, since they had lost all hope for Clare by this time, they turned directly to Agnes and said, "Why have you come to this place? Hurry home with us as quickly as possible."

However, when she answered that she did not want to leave her sister Clare, one of the knights ferociously flung himself on her and, barring no punches or blows, tried to drag her off by the hair while the others shoved her and pulled her by the arms. At this point, as the young girl was literally being snatched from the Lord's hands, she cried out as if she were being captured by lions, "Help me, dear sister! Don't let them take me away again from Christ the Lord!" Now then, as these violent marauders were dragging the recalcitrant girl down the side of the mountain, ripping her clothes and marking their path with patches of her hair, Clare tearfully prostrated herself in prayer, beseeching the Lord to grant her sister perseverance and begging divine power to overcome the strength of those men.

26. Right then and there, Agnes' body, which was stretched out on the ground, seemed to become so heavy that all those men exerting all their strength were completely unable to carry her beyond a certain stream. Other men even ran over from the fields and vineyards to help them, but there was no way that they could lift that body from the ground. Since they were forced to give up their attempts, they jokingly commented on this strange occurrence, "She must have eaten lead all night. No wonder she weighs so much!" Moreover, Sir Monaldo, her paternal uncle, who was so angry that he wanted to thrash her ruinously with his fist, was

suddenly struck by such an agonizing pain in the hand he had raised against her that for a long time afterwards he was tormented by atrocious pain. After this long trial, Clare finally arrived and she begged her family to withdraw from this conflict and entrust Agnes, who lay there semiconscious, to her care. The minute those people had gone bitterly on their way, Agnes cheerfully got up and, now enjoying the cross of Christ that she had defended in this first battle, dedicated herself to serving God forever. Blessed Francis himself then cut her hair and, together with her sister, trained her in the way of the Lord. Nevertheless, since the magnificent perfection of Agnes' life cannot be described in a just a few simple words, let's return to Clare.

Another miracle of the defeat of the demons.

27. It is no wonder that Clare's prayers were powerful against the evil of men, since they were even able to ward off demons. Once, a pious woman from the diocese of Pisa went to the monastery to give thanks to God and to St Clare for freeing her of five demons through Clare's intercession. As the demons were being exorcised, they even admitted that St Clare's prayers had infuriated them and forced them to leave the vessel they had possessed. Thus it was with good reason that Pope Gregory placed such extraordinary faith in the prayers of this saint, as he himself had experienced their power. In fact, when he encountered any new difficulties that happened to arise, not only as Bishop of Ostia and also after he had been elevated to the papacy, he often wrote to this virgin, asking for her intercession and then he would also acknowledge her help. This was certainly a highly unusual form of humility that deserved to be imitated, for the Vicar of Christ himself was asking Christ's handmaiden for her help, entrusting himself to her power. He was truly aware of what love could do and knew that the door to the Lord's consistory was opened wide to let in pure virgins. So, if the King of

heaven could give Himself over to their burning love, what could He possibly want to refuse them in their devout prayers?

Of her marvelous devotion to the sacrament of the altar.

28. The magnitude of Blessed Clare's devoted affection towards the sacrament of the altar is demonstrated by the effects it had. During that serious illness that confined Clare to her pallet, she asked to be lifted up and sustained with bolsters[68]. Then, once she was seated, she wove very delicate fabrics[69] that she used to make more than fifty sets of corporals[70], which she wrapped in silk or in purple cloth and sent to various churches throughout the valley and hills of Assisi. Whenever she was about to receive the Body of Christ, first she shed hot tears and then trembled as she approached it, for she had no less fear of Him when He was con-

---

[68] According to Sister Pacifica and Sister Cecilia, since Clare did not have any pillows, she had the sisters place rolls of cloth behind her back (*Proceedings*).

[69] Apparently, Clare spun the cloth while the other sisters prepared the fabric on a loom.

[70] Sister Francesca testified that she had counted fifty sets of corporals, the small linen cloths put on the center of the altar on which the Eucharist is placed (*Proceedings*).

cealed in the Sacrament than as Ruler of heaven and earth.

Of a truly miraculous comfort that the Lord granted her in her illness

29. She always called Christ to mind throughout her illness, so Christ likewise visited her in her weakness. At the moment during the Christmas celebration in which the world rejoices with the angels over the newborn Baby, all the sisters went to the oratory for Matins, leaving their Mother alone with her affliction. Starting to think about Baby Jesus and greatly regretting the fact that she could not be there in person to sing His praise, she sighed, "Lord God, here I am all alone in this place." Suddenly those marvelous harmonies that were being sung in the Church of St Francis began to resound in her ears. She could hear the friars singing psalms and joyfully followed the cantors' melodies, perceiving even the sounds of the instruments. This place was certainly not close enough to have made it humanly possible to hear these things unless the sounds of that solemnity had been sent to her by divine will or the human potential of her hearing had been strengthened enormously. Indeed, what even surpasses this auditory miracle is the fact that she was permitted to see Jesus' creche. Thus, when her daughters went to her the next morning, Blessed

Clare said to them, “Blessed be our Lord Jesus Christ, who did not abandon me, even though you did. Through our Lord’s intercession, I actually heard the entire Mass that was celebrated last night in Church of St Francis.

Of her fervent love for the Cross.

30. Weeping over the Lord's Passion was quite familiar to her and, while at times she drew the bitterness of myrrh from His sacred wounds, other times she drank in much sweeter joy. She became highly inebriated on the tears of Christ's Passion and often her mind portrayed for her the One whom love had impressed so profoundly upon her heart. She taught her novices to mourn Christ crucified and everything that she taught through her words she also demonstrated through her actions. Consequently, it often happened that as she was exhorting this love in particular to them, her tears would start to flow before the words were even out of her mouth. Of all the canonical hours, Sext and None[71] usually affected her with the greatest feeling of penitence, making her want to sacrifice herself with our sacrificed Lord. One time in particular, as she was praying in her cell at None, the devil struck her on the jaw, making one of her eyes completely bloodshot and bruising her cheek. In order to nourish her soul uninterruptedly on the delights

[71] Sext were the prayers said at noontime, whereas None indicated the prayers recited in midafternoon.

of the Cross, moreover, in her prayers she frequently meditated on the five wounds of the Lord. She learned the Divine Offices of the Cross as she had been taught by Francis, who loved the Cross, and usually recited these prayers the same way he did. She cinched a cord tied with thirteen knots beneath her clothes right next to her skin as a secret reminder of the Savior's wounds.

Her commemoration of the Lord's Passion.

31. Once, towards evening on the day commemorating the Last Supper when the Lord "loved his own ... to the end"[72], Clare sadly and mournfully closed herself off in her cell as the time of the Lord's agony approached. Joining our praying Lord in prayer, her "heart filled with sorrow to the point of death"[73] on account of His sadness and, feeling more and more dismayed by His capture and derision, she tossed and turned on her bed. Thus, all that night and the entire next day she was so completely absorbed, so beside herself, that, never blinking an eye and ever intent on that sole vision, she seemed to be nailed with Christ [74] and was

---

[72] Jn 13, 1.
[73] Mt 26, 38 and Mk 14, 34.
[74] Gal 2, 19.

completely without sensation. A daughter who was very close to her went back and forth to her many times to see if she wanted anything, but she always found her in the same position. When Saturday evening arrived, this devoted daughter lit a candle and, through a wordless gesture, reminded her Mother of St Francis' injunction, because he had ordered her not to let a day go by without food. Therefore, as the woman stood before her, as if she had just returned from somewhere else, Clare uttered to her, "Why do we need candles? Isn't it daytime?" "Mother," she responded, "a night has passed and another day as well, and now it is nighttime again". And Clare said to her, "My dearest daughter, blessed be this sleep, which has been granted to me after I had yearned for it for so long. But don't tell anyone about this slumber for as long as I live"!

Of the various miracles that she worked in the name of the Cross.

32. The beloved Cross rewarded its lover and she who burned with such great love for the mystery of the cross was illuminated by the power of the cross through evident miracles. In fact, whenever she made the sign of the life-giving cross over the sick, she amazingly put their illnesses to flight. I will mention just a few of these numerous episodes. A brother named Stephen, who had gone mad, was sent to Lady Clare by St Francis so that she could make the sign of the most holy cross over him, for Francis was truly aware of her extraordinary perfection and venerated her great virtue. His daughter thus obediently made the sign of the cross over the man as her Father had ordered and then she let him sleep a little in the place where she herself usually prayed. When he awoke from this nap just a short time later, however, he was healthy and thus returned to his Father cured of his insanity[75].

33. A three-year old child named Mattiolo from the city of Spoleto had pushed a pebble up his nostrils. No one was able to remove it from his nose, nor was the child able to sneeze it out. He was in

[75] See Cause of Canonization, n. 18.

great danger and agony when he was brought to Lady Clare, but as soon as she made the sign of the cross over him, he immediately expelled the pebble and was saved[76].

Another child from Perugia, whose entire eye was clouded over by a spot, was brought to the Saint of God. Touching the boy's eye, she marked it with the sign of the cross and said, "Bring him to my mother so that she too can make the sign of the cross over him." Her mother, and I mean Lady Ortolana, had followed her little plant, entering the Order after her daughter and in her widowhood, she had withdrawn to the garden with the virgins to serve the Lord. Consequently, as soon she too had made the sign of the cross over the child's eye, it was immediately purified of the spot and the boy was able to could see clearly and accurately. Clare thus asserted that the boy had been delivered through her mother, whereas her mother declined the burden of such praise in favor of her daughter, declaring that she herself did not deserve it.

34. One of the nuns named Benvenuta[77] had been afflicted for almost twelve years with a fistulous sore under her arm that oozed pus through five openings. Feeling sorry for her, Clare, the vir-

---

[76] See *Proceedings* for the testimony of Sister Benvenuta of Perugia.

[77] This was Benvenuta di Diambra, who was from Assisi. She was the eleventh witness at the *Proceedings*.

gin of God, applied her special treatment of the healing sign and as soon as this sister had been touched with the sign of the cross, she was completely cured of her age-old ulcer. Another nun named Amata had been bed-ridden for thirteen months, bloated with dropsy, and was also tormented by a cough and an ache in her side. Moved with pity for her, Lady Clare resorted to the sublime test of her medicinal arts: she made the sign of the cross over her in Christ's name and immediately restored her to complete health[78].

35. Another one of Christ's handmaidens, a native of Perugia, had lost her voice two years before and could barely express herself intelligibly[79]. She spent the entire night of Our Lady's Assumption anxiously awaiting daybreak, since it had been revealed to her in a vision that Lady Clare would cure her. At first light, she hurried to her Mother, requested the sign of the cross and recovered her voice as soon as the sign was made.

A nun named Christiana[80], who had long suffered from deafness in one ear, had tried many remedies for her affliction, but they were all in vain. Lady Clare compassionately made the sign of the

---

[78] Amata herself testified to this miracle (*Proceedings*).

[79] The woman referred to here was Benvenuta of Perugia, who testified about her own cure (*Proceedings*).

[80] Christiana of ser Christian di Paride recounted her miraculous cure (Proceedings).

cross over her head and touched her ear and the nun instantly got her hearing back.

In the monastery, there were a number of ill sisters who were tormented by various afflictions[81]. As was the custom, Clare went in with her usual medicine and immediately cured five sisters by making the sign of the cross five times. It is evident from these events that rooted within the virgin's breast was the tree of the cross, which not only nourished souls with its fruit but also offered external medicine through its leaves.

---

[81] Jn 5, 3.

Of the daily training of the sisters.

36. Since she served as a teacher to the unlettered, she was like the woman who led the young girls in the palace of the great King[82], training them so capably and protecting them so charitably that no words can fully express what she did. First of all, she taught them to drive all confusion from the dwelling place of the mind, so that they could reside continuously within the recesses of the Lord. She taught them to stop being dominated by their physical love of family and to forget their fathers' homes in order to become pleasing to God. She urged them to ignore the needs of their fragile bodies and to control carnal frivolities through the dominance of reason. She showed them that the insidious adversary lays hidden traps for pure souls and that he tempts saints in one way but worldly people in another. Finally, she wanted them to attend to manual work at set times so that, in accordance with the wishes of their Founding Father[83],

---

[82] This is an allusion to Old Testament passages.

[83] According to the Rule of the Friars Minor and the Rule of St Clare, no work should be so great that it could detract from the spirit of prayer.

they would immediately be warmed nevertheless through prayer and, by abandoning sluggish carelessness, would shake off cold lack of devotion through the fire of holy love. In no other place was there any greater observance of silence[84], nor in any other place did the proof and substance of utmost decorum enjoy greater favor. There was no flood of words here to reflect flighty souls, nor was there any verbal insensitivity to demonstrate thoughtlessness in love. Indeed, the teacher herself, a woman of few words, compressed the complex subjects of the mind into succinct remarks.

[84] In his *First Life*, Thomas of Celano noted that due to the daily silence kept at St Damian's, several of the sisters had forgotten how to speak!

Of her readiness to listen to the word of the Gospel

37. She made sure that, through devout preachers, her daughters were nourished with the word of God, of which she herself took the lion's share[85]. Since she was overcome with joy whenever she heard the holy gospel, she took such delight in remembering her Jesus that one time, while Brother Philip of Adria was preaching, a beautiful child appeared beside the virgin Clare and cosseted her during most of the sermon, displaying his pleasure. When she saw this apparition, Clare, who was worthy of this maternal vision, experienced an inexplicable feeling of sweetness. Furthermore, although Clare was not a lettered person, she nevertheless enjoyed hearing a sermon in good Latin and was convinced that concealed within the shell of the words is the core, which she penetrated with subtle comprehension and very heartily enjoyed. She was able to draw what is good for the soul from the speech of any orator, for she was aware that sometimes it is just as astute to pluck the flower

[85] Although Clare usually took less than her share at mealtimes, she was greedy when it came to her spiritual nourishment and was more than willing to take the biggest portion.

from a sharp thorn-bush as it is to eat the fruit of an excellent tree. Once, since Pope Gregory had forbidden the friars to go to the Women's monastery without permission, this pious mother regretted that the sisters would receive the food of the sacred doctrine even more rarely than before. She said with a sigh, "Since those who nourished our souls have been taken away from us, let's do without anything else from the friars as well." She immediately sent all the friars back to the Minister, because she did not want to keep those almoners to provide bread for their bodies if they no longer had almoners to provide bread for their souls. As soon as Pope Gregory got word of this, however, he immediately had the Minister General lift this ban.

Of her great charity towards her sisters.

38. This esteemed Abbess not only loved her daughters' souls but she also took care of their bodily needs with wonderfully zealous love. In fact, in the cold of night she often covered them up again herself and wanted those she had noted were unable to observe their usual severity to follow a milder routine. If one of them were troubled by temptation or, as sometimes happened, if one of them were overcome with sadness, she would call her aside and tearfully console her. Sometimes she would lay herself down at the feet of the sick so she

could relieve their sharp pain with her motherly caresses. And these daughters, who were grateful for her help, rewarded her with their complete devotion. They, on the other hand, understood the love their mother showed them, respected their teacher's superior office, followed their foundress' upright behavior and admired the privilege of sanctity of the bride of God in all its shades of meaning.

Of her illnesses and prolonged weakness.

39. By this time, she had been running her race through the stadium of the most sublime poverty for forty years and, preceded by numerous illnesses, was now approaching the prize of her heavenly calling. Since she had forced her physical being to succumb to the austerity of penance during her early years, in her later years she fell victim to severe illness. It was almost as if, just as she had been enriched through the merit of her works while she was still healthy, she would now be enriched in illness through the merits of suffering. Indeed, "in weakness, power reaches perfection" [86]. And the way in which her marvelous virtue was brought to perfection in weakness is proven in particular by the fact that throughout her prolonged twenty-eight-year affliction, there was never a murmur nor a complaint from her. Rather, holy dialogue and gratitude were always on her lips. Although she was so oppressed by the burden of her illness that she seemed to be hastening towards death, God chose to delay her passing until she was deservedly exalted by the Roman Church, whose creature and special daughter

[86] 2 Cor 12, 9.

she was. At this point, her daughters' hearts were pierced by unfathomable sorrow because the Holy Father and the cardinals had been held up in Lyon and Clare was starting to take a turn for the worse.

40. Soon, however, the following vision appeared to one of Christ's handmaidens who had been consecrated in the Benedictine Monastery of St Paul[87]. This sister felt as though she were together with her sisters at St Damian's to help Lady Clare in her illness and that Clare herself were lying on a precious bed. As they wept and tearfully awaited Blessed Clare's death, a majestic woman appeared at the foot of the bed and spoke to the crying women, saying, "Daughters, don't weep over one who will continue to live: she cannot die until the Lord has come with his disciples." A short time later, who should arrive in Perugia but the Roman Curia itself[88]. As soon as the Bishop of Ostia heard that she had taken a turn for the worse, he hurried down from Perugia to visit the bride of Christ: through his official position, he had acted as a father to her, he had nourished her through his attention and had been her ever-devoted friend through the purest of love[89]. He nourished the sick woman

---

[87] That is, at the monastery near Bastia where Clare herself had gone immediately after taking the veil at the Porziuncola.

[88] Various sources indicate that the Pope arrived in Perugia on November 5, 1251.

[89] By the time the *Legend of St Clare* was completed, Alex-

with the Sacrament of the Body of Christ and then also nourished the others through the exhortations contained in his beneficial sermon. Clare tearfully beseeched the Father simply to watch over her soul and the souls of the other Sisters in Christ's name. However, she did request one particular favor of him and that is, she implored the Pope and the Cardinals to confirm the privilege of poverty. As faithful guardian of their Order, he gave her his verbal promise, which he later fulfilled. When the year was out, the Pope moved from Perugia to Assisi together with the cardinals so that the foregoing vision about the Saint's passing could be fulfilled. In fact, the Supreme Pontiff, who is beyond mere humanity but is still on this side of divinity, represents the figure of the Lord, and the cardinals are close to his side in the temple of the Church militant.

---

ander IV had become pope. At the time of her death, however, he was still Cardinal Reginald of Segni, Bishop of Ostia and Protector of the Order of St Damian's. The visit referred to here took place on September 8, 1252 and it was followed by the letter dated the 16th, in which he assured Clare about the Diploma of Poverty. This same letter was later included in the Apostolic Letter *Solet annuere*, which was written by Innocent IV.

How Lord Innocent visited the sick woman, absolving and blessing her.

41. By this time, Divine Providence was accelerating the fulfillment of its designs for Clare: Christ was accelerating this poor pilgrim's sublimation towards the palace of the kingdom of heaven. By this time, with all her heart she yearned and desired "to be freed from this body under the power of death"[90] and to see Christ, who had been poor on earth and whom she had followed with all her heart in this same poverty, as He reigned in His eternal abode. And so a new weakness accumulated in those sacred limbs that had already been worn down by her old affliction: this not only indicated that the Lord's call was at hand but it also prepared her way to perpetual health. Together with the cardinals, our dearly departed Pope Innocent IV rushed to visit Christ's handmaiden and, just as he had approved her life over and above the life led by the women of our times, he did not hesitate to honor her death with his papal presence. As soon as he entered the monastery, he went to her litter, placing his hand near the sick woman so she could kiss it. She took his hand in rapture, and then also

[90] Rm 7, 24.

asked the Pope for his foot so that she could kiss it in reverence. This courteous lord got up on a wooden stool and offered her his foot. She kissed the top and the sole of his foot and then devoutly placed it against her cheek.

42. Finally, her face looking angelic, she asked the Supreme Pontiff for the remission of all her sins. He exclaimed, "Would that I had just as much need of pardon!" Then he gave her his bountiful blessing, granting her full absolution. After everyone had gone and she had received the sacred Host at the hands of the provincial Minister, she lifted her eyes towards heaven and folded her hands in prayer, tearfully saying to her sisters, "Praise the Lord, my daughters, for today Christ has granted me this blessing that all of heaven and earth could not repay! Today I have received the Most High himself," she explained, "and I have been allowed to see his Vicar."

How she responded to her weeping sister-german.

43. Her daughters, who were soon to be orphans, stood about their Mother's bed, their souls "pierced with a sword" of sharp pain[91]. Sleep did

---

[91] Lk 2, 35.

not turn them away nor did hunger uproot them. They forgot their beds and their dinner table and only delighted in weeping day and night. One of them was the pious virgin Agnes, who, drunk on salty tears, begged her sister not to abandon her. Clare answered her, "My dearest sister, it is God's will that I go away, but stop weeping because you too will come to the Lord shortly after me and the Lord will comfort you greatly before I leave you.

Of her final passage and what occurred then and appeared in visions.

44. Towards the end, she was in agony for a number of days and during that time the faith and devotion of the people grew. Like a true saint, she was honored every day with visits from cardinals and prelates with their retinues. And this event is marvelous to relate: although she was unable to eat any food for seventeen days, the Lord reinvigorated her with such strength that, in service to Christ, she comforted all those who went to see her. In fact, while good-natured Brother Reginald was encouraging her to be patient through the prolonged torture of such serious illness, she lightheartedly answered him, "My dearest brother, ever since I learned of the grace of my Lord Jesus Christ through his servant Francis, I have never found any pain or penance or penance or illness that could afflict me."

45. Then, since the Lord was approaching and she had already almost crossed the threshold, she wanted her priests and spiritual brothers to be near her and to recite the Lord's Passion and passages of sacred scripture. As soon as she saw that among them was Brother Juniper, the Lord's famous soldier who often uttered the fiery words of God, she

was overcome with renewed joy and asked him if he had anything new to relate about the Lord. He no sooner opened his mouth than the flaming sparks of his words spewed forth from the furnace of his ardent heart and the virgin of God found great comfort in his parables. At last, she turned to her grieving daughters to ask them to be committed to the poverty of the Lord and, praising the Lord, she reminded them of divine blessing. She blessed her devoted men and women and asked that all the Women of the poor monasteries, both present and future, be blessed. Who could describe the rest without weeping? Two of Blessed Francis' companions were present. One of them, Angelo, who was in pain himself, consoled the afflicted woman, while the other one, Leo, kissed the litter of the woman who was about to pass away.

These desolate daughters manifested their sorrow over the departure of their mother and tearfully accompanied the passage of the one whom soon they would see no longer. They very bitterly regretted that all their consolation would be leaving with her and that, left "in this vale of tears"[92], they would no longer be comforted by their teacher. This was very difficult for them, for only shame could keep them from inflicting pain on themselves and this aching sorrow was rendered even more vi-

---

[92] Ps 83, 7.

olent by the fact that it was not allowed to be dissipated through extreme signs of grief. Claustral severity required silence, but the violence of pain extracted wails and sobs. Their cheeks were swollen by their tears and there was a fresh surge of tears with every beat of their mournful hearts.

46. Speaking to her own soul, the most holy virgin softly said to it, "Go peacefully, because you will have good guidance on the way. Go," she continued, "because He who created you and blessed you, always watching over you like a mother watches over her child, has also loved you tenderly." Then she added, "Bless you, Lord, who created me." When one of the sisters asked her to whom she was speaking, she answered, "I am speaking to my blessed soul." Nor was that glorious guide far away. In fact, turning to one of her daughters, she asked, "O daughter, can you see the King of glory that I see?" And "the hand of the Lord came upon" yet another sister[93]: her eyes were allowed to glimpse a happy vision through her tears. Pierced by the arrow of intense sorrow, she glanced over towards the entryway to the house and saw that entering through the doorway was a retinue of virgins all dressed in white and wearing golden

[93] Adapted from Ez 1, 3. Although Amata was the one addressed by Clare about the King of glory, it was Benvenuta who had the vision of the virgins.

crowns on their heads. Moving ahead of the others was one who was brighter than all the rest and her crown, which looked like an embroidered thurible on top, radiated so much splendor that night itself was turned into day inside the house. She went towards the bed where her Son's bride lay and, bending over her very lovingly, gave her the gentlest embrace. The virgins offered her an incredibly beautiful pallium[94] and, rushing to serve her, they covered Clare's body with it and adorned the room[95].

The day after the feast of St Lawrence [96], that most holy soul who had been worthy of being crowned with the laurels of eternal reward, departed this life and her spirit joyfully went to heaven, for it had been set free of the temple of the flesh. Blessed be this departure from the valley of misery, which became her entrance into a life of beatitude! Instead of eating spare meals, she was now rejoicing at the table of the heavenly host, and instead of living among lowly ashes, she was delight-

---

[94] A pallium is a circular white wool band with pendants that is worn over the shoulders by popes or archbishops.

[95] According to the highly vivid and detailed description offered by Benvenuta of Diambra, "the cloth was so thin that ... although this lady was covered by it, she could be seen beneath it nonetheless" (*Proceedings*).

[96] Even today, the feast of St Lawrence, patron saint of Perugia, is commemorated on August 10th. The city of Assisi celebrates the feast of its patron saint, St Rufinus, on August 11th.

ing in the kingdom of heaven and now wore the stole of eternal glory.

How the Roman Curia attended the virgin's funeral rites together with crowds of people.

47. Word of the virgin's death immediately shook the entire population of the city with its incredible news. Men and women poured into the place[97] and there was such a great overflow of people that the city seemed deserted. Everyone proclaimed her a saint, everyone proclaimed her to be dear to God, and many of these words of praise were accompanied by tears. The podesta'[98] hurried down there with a multitude of knights and a legion of soldiers. That evening and throughout the night, they positioned diligent sentinels so that the precious treasure that lay in their midst would not be damaged in any way.

The next day the entire Curia came: the Vicar of Christ entered the place with the cardinals and the entire population of the city walked towards St Damian's. When it was time to celebrate the holy Sacrifice, the friars began to recite the Offices of

---

[97] The word "place" is often used in Franciscan terminology to designate a sacred spot or shrine, in this case the Monastery of St Damian's.

[98] In medieval Italy, the "podestà" was the chief town magistrate.

the Dead but the Pope immediately said that they should recite the Offices of the Virgins instead. Thus, it seemed that he wished to canonize her even before her body had been given over to burial. However, since the eminent Bishop of Ostia objected that this was a matter requiring a greater degree of consideration, the Mass for the Dead was celebrated. A short time later, after the Supreme Pontiff had been seated together with the circle of cardinals and bishops, the Bishop of Ostia took the "vanity of vanities"[99] as his theme to praise this singular despiser of vanity in a noble sermon.

48. The cardinals soon surrounded the sacred remains in pious respect and completed the ritual Offices around the Virgin's body. At last, since they considered it neither safe nor worthy to keep such a precious jewel far from its fellow citizens, her body was raised up to the sound of hymns and praise and of trumpets and solemn rejoicing and was transported in honor to the Church of St George. In fact, this was the place in which the body of the holy father, Francis, was first laid to rest. It was almost a sort of omen, as if the one who had marked her way of life for her while she was alive had also prepared her resting place in death. Later, at the Virgin's burial, there was a large throng of people who were praising God and saying, "This woman

[99] Eccl 1, 2.

who receives so much honor from men on earth is truly a saint, she truly reigns in glory with the angels! Intercede with Christ on our behalf, o Abbess of the Poor Women, who guided countless people in penance and countless people to life." Just a few days later, Agnes, who had been called to the Lamb in marriage, followed her sister Clare to eternal delight, where both of these daughters of Zion, german by nature, in grace and in reign, eternally rejoiced in God. Thus, Agnes truly did receive that consolation that Clare had promised her before she passed away. Indeed, as she had been preceded by her sister in leaving the world to follow the cross, even as Clare was already beginning to shine through various signs and miracles, Agnes also followed her in the light that soon ends to reawaken in God. This was granted to her by our Lord Jesus Christ who, with the Father and the Holy Spirit, lives and reigns forever and ever. Amen.

PART TWO

Of St Clare's posthumous miracles.

49. The things that comprise their saintly behavior and the perfection of their works truly represent marvelous signs of the Saints and offer venerable proof of their miracles. "John may never have performed a sign"[1], yet those who worked miracles should not be considered any holier than John. Therefore if the warmth and devotion of the people were the only things required to testify to the sublime perfection of this holy virgin, Clare, then praise of her life would suffice. During her lifetime, Clare became famous through her merits and now that she had been taken into the abyss of perpetual clarity, the light of her miracles had given her great fame to the very ends of the earth. I am obliged by sincere and sworn truth to describe many of these miracles, but their abundance also forces me to omit a great number of them.

---

[1] Jn 10, 41, referring to John the Baptist.

Of the people possessed by the devil that she freed.

50. A young boy named Giacomino of Perugia did not seem to be ill, but appeared instead to be possessed by a horrible demon. In fact, sometimes he would throw himself into the fire in desperation, other times he would writhe on the ground and yet other times he would gnaw at stones until his teeth broke, so that he miserably wounded his head and bloodied his body. Twisting his mouth and sticking out his tongue, he would then curl up all his limbs with such ease that often he could wrap his legs around his neck. This so-called insanity tormented him twice a day and the strength of two people could not stop him from stripping off his clothes. Medical experts were consulted for a remedy, but no one knew what to do. Since he had been unable to find any men who could remedy such great misfortune, the boy's father, named Guidolotto, turned to the goodness of Saint Clare. "O most holy virgin," he said, "O Clare, venerated the world over, I consecrate my poor son to you and turn all my petitions over to you to beg you to cure him." He faithfully hurried to her sepulcher, bringing his son with him. Placing the child on the virgin's tomb, he obtained her help even before he had finished asking her for it. In fact, the boy was immediately cured of that insanity and was never again tormented by any similar suffering.

Another miracle.

51. Alessandrina della Fratta, who was from the Perugia diocese, was oppressed by an extremely cruel demon. He had her so completely in his power that he would make her circle like a bird over a steep cliff leading up from the riverside. Then he would make her go down along a very slender tree branch that hung out over the Tiber and hang there in midair as if she were playing games. On top of all this, because of her sins, she had completely lost the use of her left side and her hand had shriveled up, but the medications that had been tried time and time again offered no improvement. With a contrite heart, she went to the tomb of the glorious virgin Clare and, invoking her praise, was cured of that triple jeopardy with a single remedy. Indeed, her gnarled hand straightened out, the left side of her body was restored to health and she was freed of that diabolical possession. During this same period of time, another woman from the same town who went to the Saint's sepulcher was blessed by being freed of the devil and cured of various aches and pains.

The man who was cured of insanity.

52. A young Frenchman who was part of the Curia's retinue was overcome by raving madness,

which struck him dumb and contorted his body monstrously. No one could hold him down and he writhed horribly in the hands of anyone who tried to detain him. His countrymen tied him down to a bier with ropes and brought him to the Church of St Clare against his will. They placed him before her tomb and he was immediately cured completely through the faith of those who had brought him there.

Of one who was cured of epilepsy.

Valentino of Spello was so unfortunate on account of his epilepsy that six times a day, he would fall over wherever he happened to be. Furthermore, plagued by contractions in one of his legs, he was unable to walk normally. He was brought to the sepulcher of St Clare on the back of a donkey and he stayed there for two days and three nights. On the third day, without anyone touching him, his leg shook with a great uproar and he was immediately cured of both illnesses.

Of the blind man who was enlightened.

Giacomello, known as the son of Spoletina[2], had been struck blind at the age of twelve. He could follow someone if guided, but without a guide, he was unable to walk without placing himself at personal risk. Once, in fact, having been left by a young boy just a short time before, he fell

---

[2] "Spoletina" is a nickname meaning "woman of Spoleto".

down, breaking his arm and cutting his head. One night as he was sleeping near the bridge in Narni, a woman appeared to him in a dream, saying, "Giacomello, why don't you come to me in Assisi and you will be cured." And when he awoke the next morning, he tremulously related his vision to two other blind men. They answered, "We've heard that a nun died recently in Assisi and people say that her to mb is honored by the Lord through the grace of healing and many miracles!" As soon as he heard this, he set laziness aside and promptly began his journey. That night near Spoleto, he saw the same vision again. Even faster than before, he literally flew as he prepared everything so he could hurry off to save his sight.

53. As soon as he reached Assisi, he found such a great crowd of people at the virgin's mausoleum that there was no way he could get up to the tomb. He placed a stone beneath his head and, even though he was upset that he couldn't get in, he very faithfully fell asleep outside the door. There, for the third time, the voice said to him, "Giacomo, if you can get in then the Lord will bless you." So when he awoke, he tearfully pleaded with the crowds and, shouting and doubling his prayers, begged them to let him through for the love of God. As soon as they let him past, he threw off his shoes, took off his clothes and wrapped a leather thong around his neck. Humbly touching the tomb in this manner,

he dozed off. "Get up," Blessed Clare said to him, "get up, for you are cured." As soon as he got up, all blindness was shaken off and the haze over his eyes dissipated. Thanks to St Clare, as he could clearly see a glimmer of light. Praising the Lord as well as St Clare, he invited everyone to bless God for the wonder of this great prodigy.

How one man regained the use of his hand.

54. A Perugine named Buongiovanni of Martino joined his fellow citizens in their war against the town of Foligno. Some heavy skirmishes were fought here and there and a blow from a stone gave him a serious fracture on his hand. In his desire to be healed, he spent a large amount of money on doctors, but no medical treatment could restore the use of his hand, which was completely powerless to do any kind of work. Thus, he was so upset about being forced to suffer the burden of that right hand, over which he essentially had no control, and about being deprived of its use that he often thought it would be better to have it amputated. Then, after hearing what the Lord had deigned to demonstrate to him through His servant Clare, he made a vow and went to the virgin's sepulcher. He offered her a wax hand and lay

down in front of the tomb of St Clare. Before he could even leave the church, his hand was immediately healed[3].

[3] The war between the Guelph city of Perugia and the Ghibelline city of Foligno was fought in May and June of 1254.

Of the crippled

55. Debilitated by a three-year illness, a certain Pietruccio from the castle of Bettona seemed to have become shriveled up and consumed by this prolonged ailment. Because his illness was so severe, his hips were so stiff that he was always curved over towards the ground and could barely even walk with a cane. The boy's father had tested the capabilities of many doctors, especially those who specialized in curing bone fractures. He was willing to spend all his money to heal his son, but since everyone had told him that no medical treatment existed for that illness, he turned to the new saint, about whom he had heard marvelous things. The boy was brought to the place where the precious remains of the virgin had been laid to rest and after he had been stretched out in front of the sepulcher for just a short time, he was blessed with a complete cure. In fact, he immediately got up straight and healthy, "walking, jumping about and praising God"[4] and he invited the people who had rushed over to praise St Clare.

56. There was a ten-year old boy in the villa of

[4] Acts 3, 8.

San Quirico near Assisi who was "crippled from birth"[5]. He had fragile shin-bones, his feet were turned sideways and he walked so crookedly that as soon as he got up, he would fall right down again. His mother had consecrated him to St Francis many times, but there had not been any improvement. Since she had heard that Blessed Clare shone because of her recent miracles, she brought the child to her sepulcher. Several days later, his shin-bones crackled and his limbs returned to their natural position. Thus, the blessing that St Francis had failed to grant in spite of numerous prayers was granted instead by his disciple, Clare, through divine favor.

57. A citizen of Gubbio named Giacomo of Franco had a little five-year old who had never learned to walk and in fact was completely unable to walk because his feet were so frail. This man complained about the boy as if he were a black mark against his house and a disgrace to his very family. The boy would stretch himself out on the floor and drag himself through the dust. He often wanted to get up with the help of a cane, but was unable to do so because, while nature had given him the desire to walk, it had denied him the ability. The boy's parents entrusted him to the merits of St Clare and, to borrow their expression, said

[5] Acts 3, 2.

that they wanted him to become "a man of St Clare"[6] if he were cured through her. A short time after they had made this vow, the virgin of Christ cured her man, giving the boy who had been offered to her the ability to walk. The boy's parents immediately rushed to the virgin's tomb with him and, jumping for joy, offered him to the Lord.

58. A woman named Pleneria, who was from the castle of Bevagna, was unable to walk without leaning on a cane because she had long suffered from kidney problems. However, even with the help of her cane, she could not straighten her curved body and she shuffled along as well as she could. One Friday, she had someone take her to the tomb of St Clare where, after praying with utmost devotion, she quickly obtained what she had faithfully requested. In fact, although she had been carried there by others, the following Saturday she walked home herself.

[6] This expression refers to perpetual service.

How a young girl was cured of nodes in the throat.

There was a young girl from Perugia who had long suffered greatly from nodes, or scrofula, in her throat, an illness commonly known as "king's evil"[7]. In fact, you could count twenty nodes in her throat and her neck appeared to be even larger than her head. Her mother often brought her to the tomb of the virgin Clare, where she very devoutly implored this saint's blessing. After the girl had spent an entire night before the sepulcher, sweating profusely, those nodes began to soften and to started to shift somewhat from their position. Thanks to St Clare, they gradually disappeared and not a trace of them was left.

59. One of the nuns named Andrea had a similar throat ailment while the virgin Clare was still alive. It is truly strange that there should have been such a cold soul hidden there among such hot coals and that amidst such sensible virgins there could be one who acted so foolishly[8]. In any case, one night she tried to strangle herself to the point of suffocation in order to expel that node from her mouth,

---

[7] "Scrofula" is tuberculosis of the cervical lymph nodes.
[8] Mt 25, 4.

for she wanted to overcome God's will for her. However, Clare immediately heard about it through divine inspiration. Turning to another sister, she said, "Run quickly to the basement and give Sister Andrea of Ferrara a heated egg to drink, and then bring her to me." The sister quickly found Andrea speechless and close to asphyxiation with her own hands wrapped around her neck. She lifted her up as well as she could and took her to their mother. The servant of God said to her, "You wretch, confess your thoughts to the Lord, with whom I too am well acquainted. Here, the illness you tried to cure by yourself will be cured by the Lord Jesus Christ. However, change your life for the better because you will not get up again from another illness that you are going to suffer!" This warning instilled the spirit of penance in this sister and she dramatically changed her life for the better. In any case, a short time after she had been cured of scrofula, she died of a different disease.

Of those who were liberated from the wolves.

60. The frightening cruelty of ferocious wolves often oppressed the area. These wolves even attacked people and often fed on human flesh. Now, a woman named Bona from Mount Galliano in the diocese of Assisi had just finished mourning one of her two children, who had been dragged off by the

wolves, when they attacked the second one just as savagely. In fact, while the woman was inside her house doing her chores, a wolf sank his teeth into the neck of her little boy, who had been walking outside, and dashed into the woods as fast as it could with its prey. However, as soon as they heard the boy's cries, some men who were in the vineyard shouted to his mother, "Check on your son because we just heard some strange cries." Realizing that her child had been taken by a wolf, the mother cried to the heavens and, filling the air with her screams, invoked the virgin Clare, saying, "Holy and glorious Clare, give my poor child back to me." She repeated, "Give this wretched mother her little boy or I will drown myself." In the meantime, the neighbors ran after the wolf and found that the boy had been abandoned by the wolf in the woods and that there was a dog near him, licking the boy's wounds. Initially, the wild beast had taken the boy by biting him on the neck but then, in order to carry off its prey more easily, the wolf had stuffed the boy into its jaws by his hips, thus leaving numerous tooth marks. True to her vow, the woman soon went with her neighbors to the one who had come to her aid and, showing all the child's wounds to anyone who was willing to look, she offered great thanks to God and to St Clare.

61. In broad daylight, a young girl from the town of Cannara was sitting in a field with another woman, who had laid her head in her lap, when a

man-eating wolf hastened its furtive steps towards its prey. The young girl actually did see it but, thinking it was a dog, she was not frightened. And as she continued to toy with the other woman's hair, the cruel beast attacked her, taking her face in its open jaws and dragging its prey into the woods. The astonished woman immediately got up and, thinking of St Clare, began to shout, "Help, St Clare, help. I entrust this girl to your care!" And at last – marvelous to relate – the girl who was being carried off in the wolf's jaws began to inveigh against it, saying, "You thief! How dare you carry me any further when I have been entrusted to such a great Virgin?" Confused by this tongue lashing, it immediately placed the girl gently on the ground and hurried off like a thief who has been caught in the act.

Of the canonization of St Clare, virgin

62. During the time that he was seated on Peter's chair, Pope Alexander IV[9], most clement prince and friend of all sainthood, presided over the Religious and was the solid mainstay of the religious Orders. Since word of this Virgin's marvels had spread far and wide and the fame of her virtues was growing by the day, the whole world now eagerly awaited the canonization of this splendid Virgin. At last, this Pontiff, who was virtually forced to reach a highly unusual decision[10] due to the existence of such an abundance of miracles, began the proceedings for her canonization, together with the cardinals.

The examination of her miracles was entrusted to eminent and just people and the task of discussing the magnitude of her life was also assigned. It was found that Clare had been most distinguished

---

[9] He was elected pope on December 12, 1254. It should be noted that the initial procedure had been ordered by Alexander's predecessor, Innocent IV, with his letter *Gloriosus Deus* dated October 18, 1253.

[10] This was unusual because Clare had been dead only two months when the pope started the canonization process.

in exercising all virtue during her lifetime and she was found to be praiseworthy through the true and proven miracles that took place after her death.

Thus, on the established day, the College of Cardinals gathered and the Assembly of Bishops and Archbishops convened and, in the presence of the clergy and a great multitude of the Religious and other wise and powerful people, the Supreme Pontiff stated this matter of salvation and asked the prelates for their opinions. Everyone promptly expressed their highly favorable vote and declared that they must illuminate Clare on earth, just as God had illuminated her in heaven.

Based on this premise, since the anniversary of her passing to the Lord was approaching and two years had elapsed since her death, lucky Alexander, for whom the Lord had reserved this grace, very solemnly and reverently included Clare in the catalogue of Saints before a multitude of Bishops and clergy who were assembled there. After declaring that her feast day was to be celebrated solemnly throughout the Church, he was the first one to celebrate her with utmost solemnity, together with the entire Curia. All of this took place in the main church of Anagni, in the Year of Our Lord 1255, first year of the pontificate of Pope Alexander, for the praise and glory of our Lord Jesus Christ, who lives and reigns with the Father and the Holy Spirit for ever and ever. Amen.

ARTI GRAFICHE ANTICA PORZIUNCOLA
S. MARIA DEGLI ANGELI - ASSISI

Printed october 2004 – Cannara (Pg)